AF437419

YOU ARE AMAZING!
TEACHER
Planner
Book Club

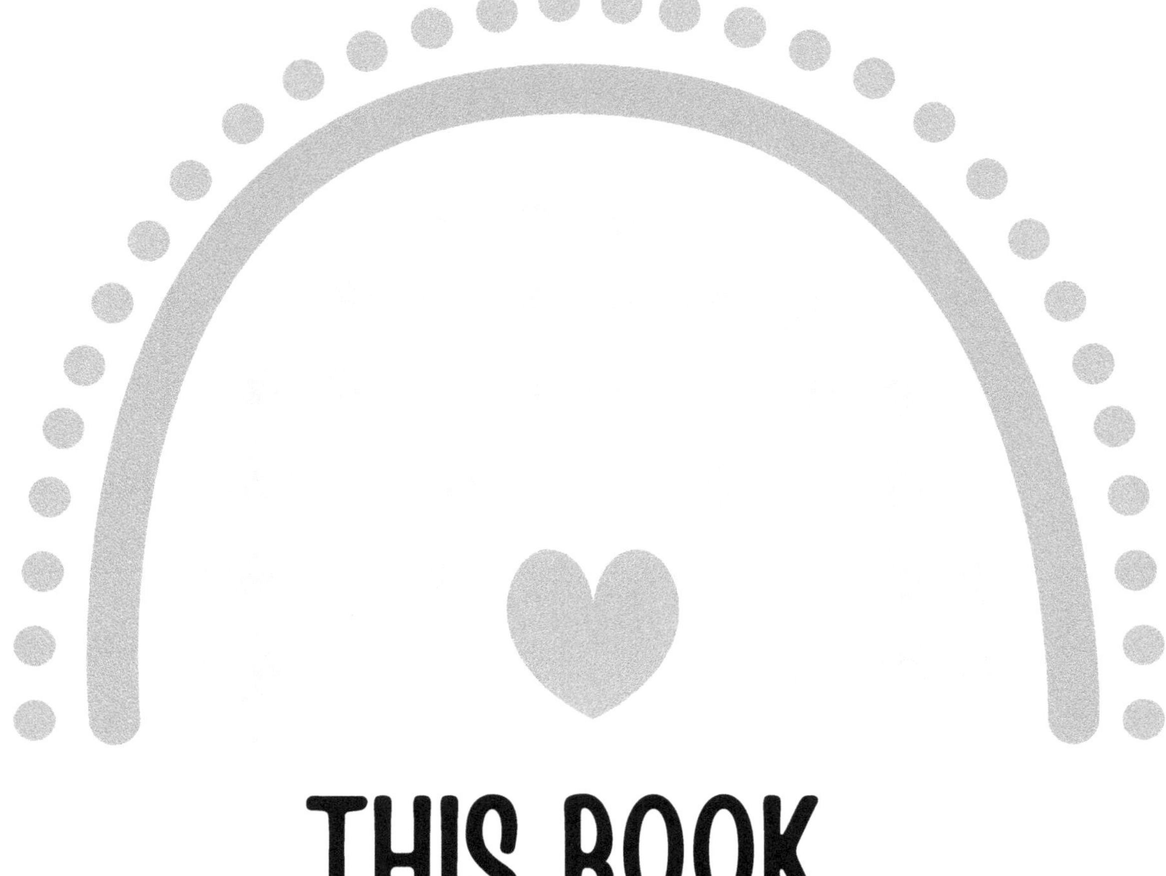

THIS BOOK

BELONGS TO

ALL ABOUT

NAME

SCHOOL

YEAR

GRADE

PHONE

WEB RESOURCES

TO-DO *list*

MY
goals

SHORT TERM PERSONAL

LONG TERM PERSONAL

SHORT TERM PROFESSIONAL

LONG TERM PROFESSIONAL

SMART
goals

S

SPECIFIC

M

MEASUREABLE

A

ATTAINABLE

R

RELEVANT

T

TIME

IMPORTANT
dates

CLASS *snapshot*

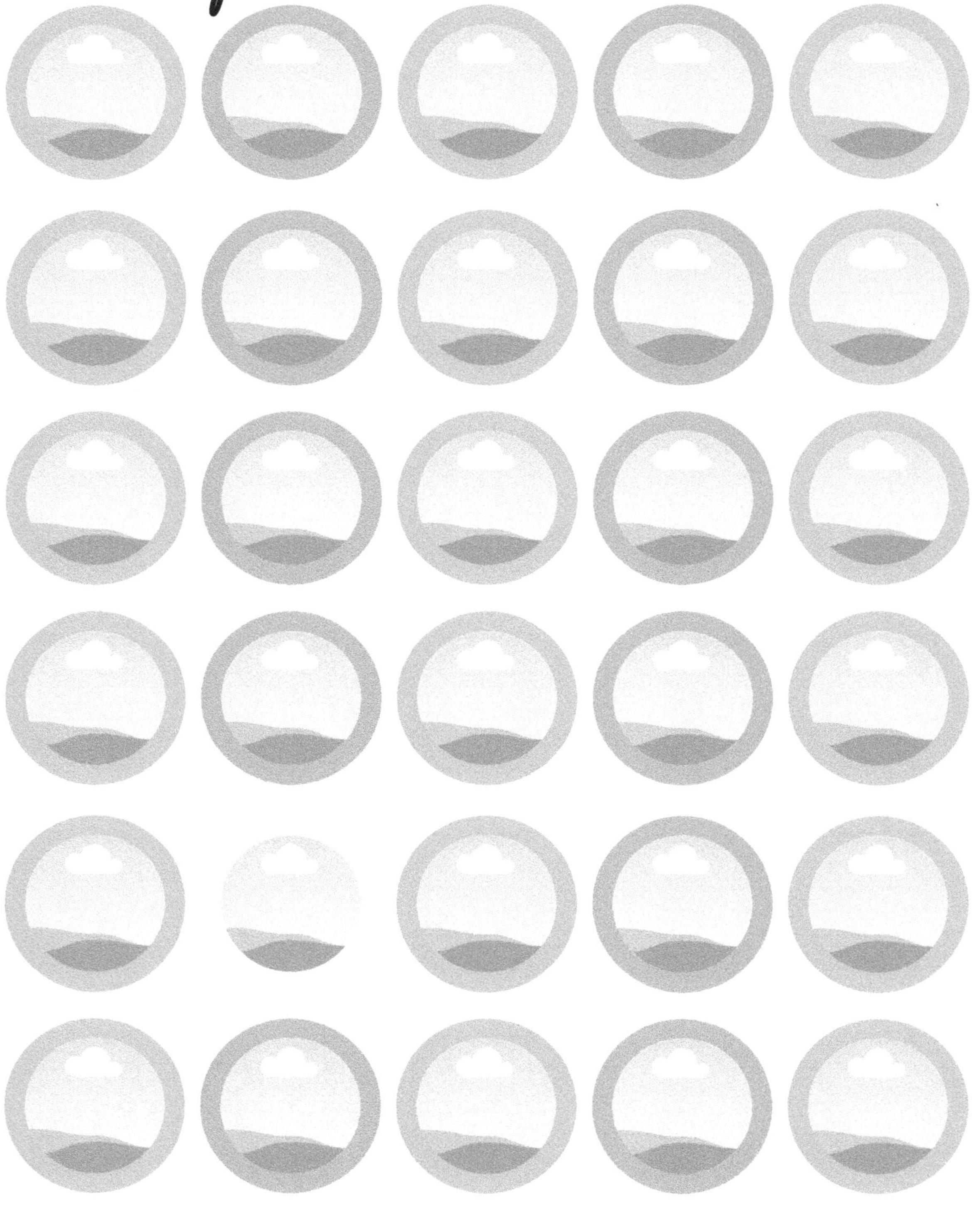

CLASS birthdays

JANUARY

FEBRUARY

MARCH

APRIL

MAY

JUNE

JULY

AUGUST

SEPTEMBER

OCTOBER

NOVEMBER

DECEMBER

HELPFUL

CLASS OVERVIEW

BEHAVIOR

NOTES

READING *groups*

WRITING
groups

MATH

groups

STUDENT
data

STUDENT	SUBJECT													

YEAR

snapshot

JANUARY

FEBRUARY

MARCH

APRIL

MAY

JUNE

YEAR *snapshot*

JULY

AUGUST

SEPTEMBER

OCTOBER

NOVEMBER

DECEMBER

JANUARY

snapshot

M	T	W	T	F

NOTES

FEBRUARY

snapshot

M	T	W	T	F

NOTES

MARCH
snapshot

M	T	W	T	F

NOTES

APRIL

NOTES

MAY

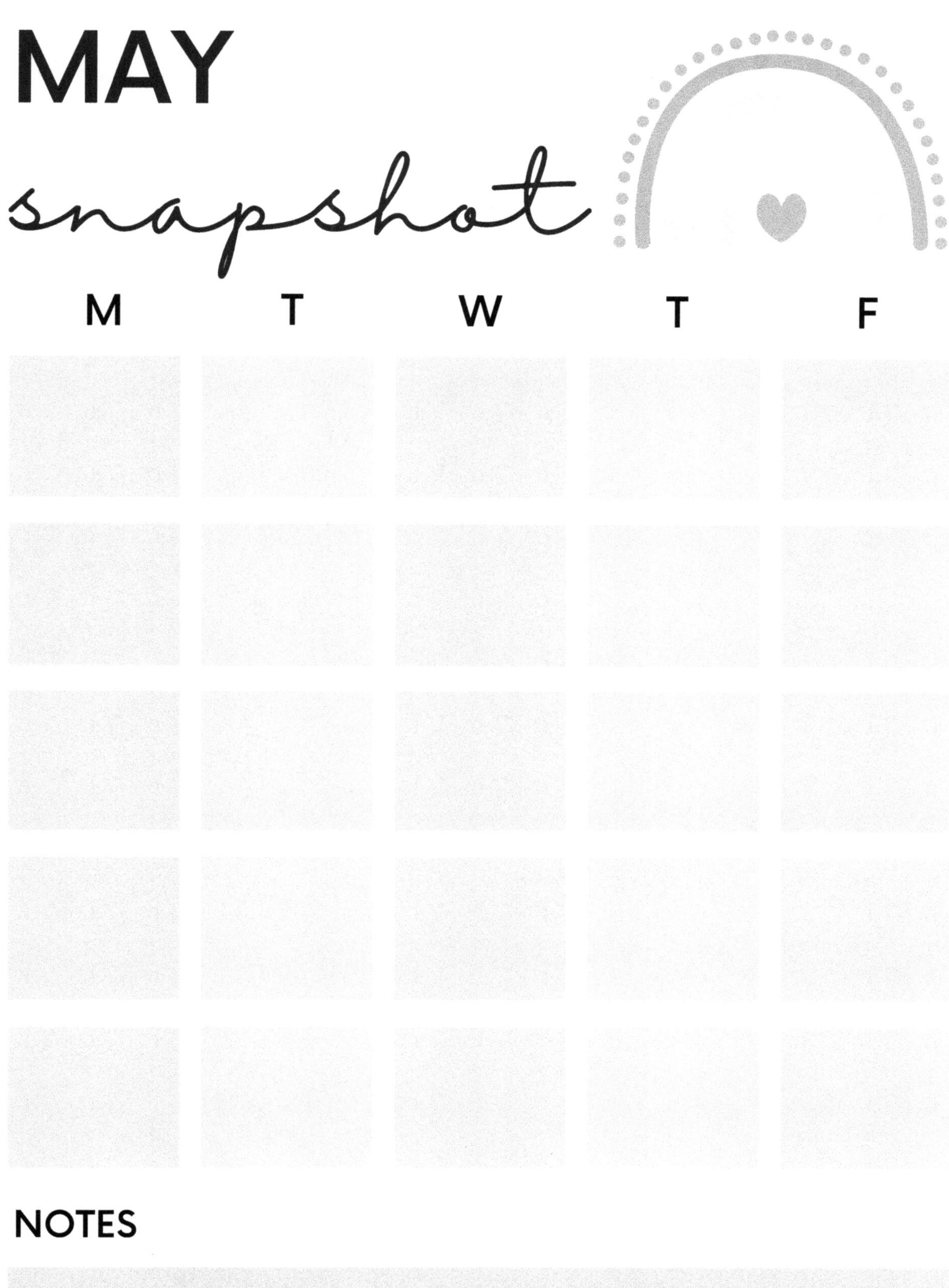

NOTES

JUNE

snapshot

M	T	W	T	F

NOTES

JULY

snapshot

M T W T F

NOTES

AUGUST

snapshot

M	T	W	T	F

NOTES

SEPTEMBER

snapshot

M	T	W	T	F

NOTES

OCTOBER

snapshot

M	T	W	T	F

NOTES

NOVEMBER

snapshot

M	T	W	T	F

NOTES

DECEMBER

snapshot

M	T	W	T	F

NOTES

SEMESTER

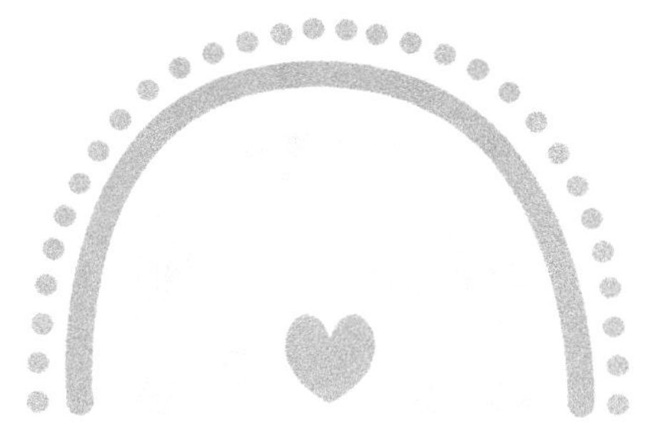

SEMESTER 1

SEMESTER 2

TERM

plan

TERM 1

TERM 2

TERM 3

TERM 4

WEEK A
timetable

	M	TU	W	TH	F
1					
2					
3					
4					
5					
6					
7					
8					

WEEK B
timetable

	M	TU	W	TH	F
1					
2					
3					
4					
5					
6					
7					
8					

WEEKLY
timetable

M	
T	
W	
T	
F	

LESSON
plan

SUBJECT

RESOURCES

LEARNING SEQUENCE

DIFFERENTIATION

NOTES

DAILY

WEEK

plan

1

2

3

4

5

6

DAILY WEEK

plan

1

2

3

4

5

6

7

DAILY

WEEK

plan

1

2

3

4

5

6

7

8

DAILY WEEK

plan

1

2

3

4

DAILY WEEK

plan

5

6

7

8

PROFESSIONAL

DATE	LEARNING FOCUS

CLASSROOM *volunteers*

ANECDOTAL

 *notes*

END

www.ingramcontent.com/pod-product-compliance
Lightning Source LLC
Chambersburg PA
CBHW041837110726
48006CB00020B/2661

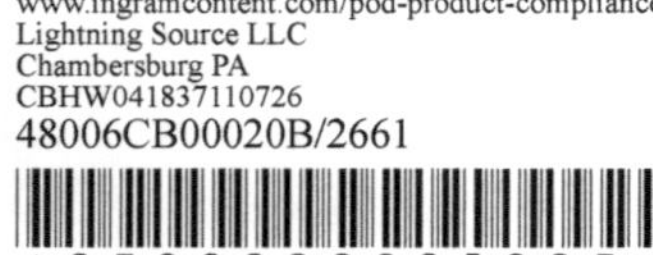